Table of Conten

Teaching Guide

Introduction

This book is one of six in a series designed to encourage the reading enjoyment of young students. Subject matter was carefully chosen to correspond to student interests. Skills were selected to reinforce understanding of the readings and to promote confidence in independent reading.

Content

The contents of each book have been drawn from seven specific categories: 1) biography, 2) amazing facts, 3) mystery and intrigue, 4) sports stars and events, 5) visual and performing arts, 6) wonders in science and nature, and 7) excerpts from mythology and literature.

The popular biographies, sports figures, and artists give students an opportunity to identify with people who are familiar to them. Those figures who are unknown to the students' experience give them clues to the wide diversity of current society in many countries. A look behind the scenes of a famous life holds a never-ending fascination.

In addition to spy stories and tales of ghostly encounters, the mystery selections often offer a puzzling situation to solve or the beginning of a story which must be completed by the reader.

Science and nature selections are chosen to generate interest in new and untapped areas of the readers' knowledge and to encourage them to explore further.

Samples of a wide variety of stories from mythology and literature have been included. It is hoped that this brief encounter with some of the great story lines will motivate the student to seek out and read the entire selection.

Skills

The skills employed in this series are drawn from traditional educational objectives. The five comprehension areas practiced in this series are: main idea, recognition of significant details, use of context clues for determining word meaning, inference, and drawing conclusions. All categories are not necessarily represented at the conclusion of each story. Questioning format varies from book to book to avoid predictability. Where space permits, a follow-through activity has been included. These are expected to lead to self-motivated reading or to valuable discussion. The activity also gives the teacher an opportunity to award extra credit.

Upon completion of each collection of stories and accompanying skill activities, students should show improvement in the areas practiced; i.e., the ability to locate, evaluate, and predict, as well as to conduct study and research.

Readability

The reading level of each book is essentially two years below the interest level. Readability levels were confirmed by the Spache formula for the lower grades and the Dale-Chall formula for the upper grades. Each book is suitable for a variety of students working at a range of reading levels. The lower readability allows older students with reading deficiencies to enjoy high-interest content with minimum frustration. The comprehension activities provide a growth opportunity for capable students as well. The high-interest content should help to motivate students at any level.

The teacher should keep in mind that supplying easy-to-read content provides a good setting for learning new skills. Thus, comprehension development can best take place where vocabulary and sentence constraints ensure student understanding. It should be obvious that the concept of main idea, as well as the nature of an inference, can be seen best where the total content of a selection is well within a reader's grasp.

Finally, the material is dedicated to the principle that the more a student reads, the better he or she reads, and the greater is the appreciation of the printed word.

Sea Rescue

A ten-year survey of world disasters shows that air crashes have increased, train wrecks have decreased, and shipwrecks have remained about the same. It is important for people involved in disasters to remain calm. In a recent shipwreck near Australia, the courage of a 13-year-old girl helped to lighten the burden of a family tragedy.

Tracey was sailing with her family — mother, father, brother — and a friend, when a storm struck. Her father, worried by the huge waves, radioed for help. Soon an oil tanker arrived to rescue them. For extra protection before they climbed onto the tanker, Tracey's father roped the family together. But as they started up the ladder, Tracey's mother slipped. At the same time, the sailboat tilted. All five people were pulled into the water and swept under the tanker. Safety had been so close. But now, certain death overtook the family.

The ropes snapped as Tracey rolled over and over under the water. Finally she and her father, the only survivors, made it to the surface. But there was no help. The tanker's captain did not see them. He had given up and sailed away. Determined to keep her father alive, Tracey wrapped arms with him. For hours she talked. She told him stories of family life over and over. Her father thought he was hearing a voice from the past, but he listened and remained conscious. At last another rescue ship arrived and pulled them from the heaving water. This disaster resulted in a firm bond of love, respect, and companionship between a father and daughter.

Main Idea
1. This story is mainly about
   a. an oil tanker.
   b. a good storyteller.
   c. a wreck at sea.

Significant Details
2. T F Disasters happen every year.
3. T F Tracey helped keep her father alive.
4. T F No one sends help when a ship goes down.
5. _____ people were lost at sea.
   a. Three   b. Five   c. Ten

Context Clues
6. A *disaster* can be (Circle the answer that does not fit.)
   a. a bad flood.   d. a family picnic.
   b. an earthquake.   e. a plane crash.
   c. a shipwreck.   f. a tornado.
7. To *increase* is to _____ .
8. To *rescue* means the same as
   a. to sail.
   b. to climb.
   c. to save.

MP3393

The Drummer of Tedworth

One of the earliest poltergeist cases ever recorded happened in Tedworth, England, in 1661. *Poltergeist* is a German word meaning "noisy ghost," and this ghost in Tedworth was certainly noisy. The weird experience started when John Mompesson, a respected magistrate, was bothered by a terrible noise. He discovered it was a beggar, William Drury, who had been walking the streets of the town for several days, beating his drum and demanding money. Mompesson and the townspeople were very annoyed by Drury, so the magistrate had the drummer arrested and his drum confiscated. William Drury was very angry. He put a spell on the Mompesson house and said he would not remove it until his drum was returned.

Then the trouble began! Night after night, drumbeats could be heard in the Mompesson house. An invisible drummer began following the Mompesson children. The drummer even beat out military songs on their beds.

Still drumming, the poltergeist began doing other things as well. The children had their shoes thrown about and their hair pulled. They were often tossed out of bed. Mrs. Mompesson found her Bible in the fireplace and ashes in the porridge bowls. A friend visiting the Mompessons found that all the money in his pockets had turned black. Everyone was shocked when John discovered his favorite horse lying on the ground with its hind leg jammed in its mouth.

Joseph Glanvill, the chaplain of King Charles II, came to investigate the mysterious happenings. He witnessed some incredible things at the Mompesson house, but could not discover a cause for the disturbances. The drummings continued for two years and then stopped as suddenly as they had started. No one has heard them since.

Main Idea

1. What did the people of Tedworth think caused the strange happenings at the Mompesson house? _____
   _____
   _____

2. Circle the words you think describe the case of the Drummer of Tedworth.
   a. eerie   c. serene   e. unnatural
   b. pleasant   d. delicate   f. terrifying

Context Clues

3. The respected *magistrate* came to town.
   a. salesman
   b. town official
   c. doctor

4. Joseph Glanvill came to *investigate* the occurrences.
   a. look into
   b. inform
   c. duplicate

5. He witnessed many *incredible* things.
   a. immature
   b. hard to see
   c. hard to believe

6. To *confiscate* means to
   a. give back something.
   b. take away something.
   c. confuse.

MP3393

Conquer the Mountain

Inside the helicopter, Mac sat quietly next to the pilot. But his excitement was growing. In minutes they would be over the drop-off point, the peak of an isolated mountain in Canada. Mac was an expert downhill skier and was always looking for a new challenge. Today he would have one. He was going to ski alone down a slope untried by other skiers. Mac had already checked the weather and snowfall for the area. He had reported his destination to the nearest ski patrol. Next he looked over his kit, map, and "beeper," which would help locate him on the mountain if he ran into trouble. He was ready when the pilot pointed to the landing site. As the helicopter hovered, Mac slid his legs over the side, snapped on his skis, grabbed his poles, and jumped.

As he hit the mountain slope at an angle, Mac quickly turned his skis to the left to slow his descent. He braked and came to a stop so he could look around. Fresh snow had fallen and Mac was nearly up to his knees in "powder." It would be fun skiing on this light powdery snow, but it would also be hard on his legs. Mac pushed off. There was no trail to follow, so Mac concentrated hard as he chose certain slopes and jumps. He went one way to miss a tree, another way to miss a rock. Back and forth, faster and faster Mac came down the slope. The air was crisp, the scenery was beautiful, and the snow was perfect. It was almost noon when Mac reached his friends at the bottom of the mountain. Although his mouth was dry and his legs were tired, Mac looked back at the mountain and grinned. He raised his poles high and said, "I did it!"

Significant Details

1. How did Mac slow his descent when he landed from the helicopter?
   a. He checked the snowfall.
   b. He grabbed his poles.
   c. He quickly turned his skis to the left.
2. What was missing on the mountain slope?
   a. rocks
   b. ski trail
   c. fresh snow

Context Clues

3. Mac was an *expert* skier.
   a. skilled
   b. fast
   c. old
4. The mountain was *isolated*.
   a. large
   b. icy
   c. alone
5. When Mac *concentrated*, he was

   _____ .

MP3393

Hot Spot

The Maori natives of New Zealand have a natural answer to energy needs. They live near the country's thermal, or heat, belt. Here, clouds of steam rise from cracks in the ground and from pools of bubbling, hot water. The Maori use water from the hot pools for washing and cooking.

Conservationists looking for sources of power are interested in geothermal energy — steam produced by volcanic rock. Electric power created by such steam has been used in Italy, Mexico, Iceland, and California. But the most successful project has been on the North Island of New Zealand. Here, steam is used to generate electricity for several nearby cities.

Engineers drill holes as deep as 4,000 feet into the earth's surface. They reach underground water heated far above the boiling point by volcanic rock. Like an oil well, the steam gushes up through steel-covered pipes. When it reaches the surface, the steam is capped. It is then sent through pipes to generating stations along the Waikato River. Geothermal areas like this never seem to run out of steam. Due to the decay of radioactive materials in the soil, the water below the surface stays hot all the time. In the U.S., some hopeful conservationists predict that by the year 2000 as much as fifteen percent of our electric power could come from geothermal energy.

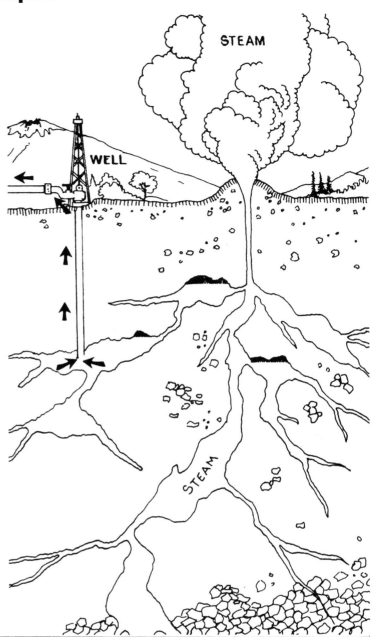

Significant Details

1. Electricity has been generated by steam
   a. for hundreds of years.
   b. on New Zealand's North Island.
   c. by Maori natives.
2. How deep can engineers drill for heated water?
   a. 4,000 feet
   b. 4,000 inches
   c. 2,000 feet
3. The people who live on New Zealand's North Island are called _____ .

Context Clues

4. Water heated above the boiling point becomes _____ .
5. *Conservationists* like to
   a. spend.
   b. drill.
   c. save.

Following Through

6. Name three ways to conserve heat in winter. _____
   _____
   _____

A Mythical Monster
(A tale from Greek mythology)

In ancient times, Thebes was an important city in Greece. But the people who lived there could neither enter nor leave the city because of the Sphinx. The Sphinx was a fierce monster with large wings, the body and tail of a lion, and the head of a woman. It sat on a rock just outside the city or flew up and down the road to Thebes. Not many people cared to visit, because as soon as the Sphinx saw someone on the road, it asked the traveler to solve a riddle. If the person failed, the monster swooped down, grasped the traveler, and quickly ate him.

One day, a young man, Oedipus, wished to visit Thebes and decided to go in spite of the monster. As he came to the gates, the Sphinx, still dripping blood from the last traveler, stopped Oedipus. "Young man," said the Sphinx, flapping its wings, "you must answer my riddle or die. What creature walks on four legs in the morning, two legs at noon, and three legs at night?"

Oedipus looked straight at the monster and said, "The answer is Man. When he is a child, he crawls on all fours; when he is halfway through life, he stands upright; and when he is old, he leans on a cane as a third leg." The answer was right. The monster screamed with rage! It was so angry that it leaped off the tall rock, crashed to the ground, and died. The happy people of Thebes opened the gates, thanked Oedipus, and soon made him their king.

Main Idea
1. The most important event in this story is
   a. Oedipus became king of Thebes.
   b. Oedipus defeated the monster.
   c. the Sphinx had a clever riddle.

Significant Details
2. Where did the Sphinx usually sit?

   _____

   _____

Context Clues
3. A *riddle* is hard to answer.
   a. creature
   b. request
   c. question

Following Through
4. Cerberus is another monster of Greek mythology that guards some gates. Find the description of this creature in a book of Greek myths. What does it look like?

   _____

   _____

   What does it guard? _____

   _____

   Which monster do you think is more dangerous? _____

   Why? _____

   _____

Sandra Day O'Connor

Sandra Day O'Connor grew up on her family's ranch in Arizona. Her earliest memories were of riding horses and rounding up cattle in the dust storms. Ranching was hard work, but Sandra was able to balance both her chores and her schoolwork. When she was eight, Sandra learned to drive a truck so that she could go out and help mend fences. She often carried a twenty-two to shoot coyotes that went after the cattle. Sandra did so well in school that by the time she was sixteen, she had graduated from high school. At Stanford University, Sandra's abilities as a law student were recognized by her professors.

After graduating magna cum laude from Stanford, she went on to take a law degree graduating third in a class of 102. Nevertheless, Sandra had trouble getting a job after graduation. Few law firms were hiring women at that time. One Los Angeles law firm did offer O'Connor a job as a legal secretary! Instead she worked for a year as county deputy attorney in San Mateo, California. Then, accompanying her soldier husband to West Germany, she became a civilian lawyer for the Quartermaster Corp. Later, back in the Phoenix area, Mrs. O'Connor had her own law firm while she raised her three sons and did community service work. In 1965, she became assistant attorney general for Arizona and four years later was appointed by the governor to fill a vacancy in the state senate. The next year O'Connor campaigned for and won the same senate seat.

Because of her hard work and intelligence, Sandra won the respect of other senators and politicians. Later, she became a judge for the state of Arizona. Her judgments were fair but tough. Her excellent work as a judge came to the attention of President Ronald Reagan, and on September 25, 1981, he appointed Sandra Day O'Connor to serve on the United States Supreme Court. She is the first woman justice ever to serve on the U.S. Supreme Court.

Main Idea
1. What did Sandra Day O'Connor become?

   _____

2. Why was her appointment significant?

   _____

   _____

Significant Details
3. Sandra studied to be a
   a. lawyer.
   b. rancher.
   c. president.
4. To become a Supreme Court justice you must
   a. win an election.
   b. be a state senator.
   c. be appointed by the President.

Context Clues
5. Sandra did both her *chores* and her schoolwork.
   a. paintings
   b. jobs
   c. hobbies
6. Sandra was *appointed* by President Reagan.
   a. named to a job
   b. elected by votes
   c. forgotten

Following Through
7. Find out more about Sandra Day O'Connor. List some important cases or rulings in which she has been involved.

Apples in the Garage

No one at the science fair was surprised when young Steven Wozniak won a blue ribbon for his addition and subtraction machine. Wozniak, or Woz, as friends called him, was a whiz at electronics. It wasn't long before Woz began applying his knowledge towards a new hobby —computers. His friend, Steven Jobs, a high school senior, worked with him day and night in the family's garage. They built an impressive computer and called it Apple I.

Always with an eye for business, Jobs convinced Woz to try to sell his computer. Woz built a good machine, but he did it for fun. As he admits, he didn't care if wires were hanging from the side of it, as long as his computer worked well. It was Jobs who enclosed the computer in a streamlined case and put it up for sale. A local computer store ordered fifty Apple computers, and Jobs and Woz were in business.

Jobs sold his van and Woz sold his two calculators in order to raise money for the needed computer parts. Their company began to grow. Woz went on to design the computer of his dreams, the Apple II with power supply, BASIC language, and color graphics. Since then, the company has developed into a large corporation.

People in the business world were impressed with the young men, Wozniak and Jobs, and with their early contributions to the computer industry.

Main Idea
1. What was the main idea of this story?

   _____

   _____

   _____

Significant Details
2. Wozniak was the engineer of the company while Jobs was in charge of
   a. the graphics.
   b. the BASIC language.
   c. the business.
3. Wozniak was very good at
   a. electronics.
   b. business.
   c. selling.

Context Clues
4. Woz and Jobs had a new *hobby*.
   a. favorite subject in school
   b. favorite thing to do in spare time
   c. game played by two people
5. The Apple Computer Company grew into a *corporation*.
   a. computer industry
   b. legend
   c. large group of people in business

Inference
6. BASIC language means the computer
   a. will understand you if you talk to it.
   b. is suited for working fairly easy programs.
   c. can only speak in one language.

Chessie

Are monsters real? Most people would probably laugh and explain, "Monsters are just creatures invented for stories to scare little children," but a farmer named Goodwin Muse might disagree. Muse was walking along a beach with five friends when he saw an actual sea monster. That summer, thirty other people also saw the incredible monster.

Chessie, the nickname given to the monster, swims the Chesapeake Bay near Washington, D.C. From a distance, Chessie looks like a long telephone pole floating in the water. Mr. Muse described her as being as round as a quart jar. He said from where he stood, her head appeared to be bigger than his hand. At first, scientists at the Virginia Institute of Marine Science thought Chessie was probably some kind of large tropical snake. The main question was how a snake adapted to warm waters could survive so far from its natural habitat. If enough evidence is gathered, scientists may soon have their answer.

Recently Chessie was sighted again. This time a man and his family spotted Chessie in the bay behind their house in Baltimore. The man quickly went for his video camera recorder and filmed Chessie as she swam by. With the help of records such as this film, scientists may be able to classify Chessie.

Inference
1. Why is Chessie described as a monster?

   _____

   _____

2. What do you think Chessie is? Explain.

   _____

   _____

   _____

   _____

Context Clues
3. The snake was far from its natural *habitat*.
   a. enemy
   b. habits
   c. home

4. A sea monster was *sighted*.
   a. troubled
   b. seen
   c. survived

8

MP3393

Master Spy

America was enjoying a time of peace. But William Donovan, a distinguished World War I veteran, was convinced that World War II was fast approaching. He went overseas to find out for himself. Donovan visited many warring countries and observed their new weapons and fighting tactics.

When the Japanese invaded Pearl Harbor in 1941, almost everyone seemed surprised except Bill Donovan. President Roosevelt turned to Bill for help. On June 13, 1942, the Office of Strategic Services (OSS) was created. As the director of OSS, Bill immediately began recruiting a variety of agents. Teachers, actors, thieves, millionaires, photographers, and deep sea divers were employed to work undercover for the OSS. Donovan parachuted his people into any area where the enemy was attacking.

Bill's agents worked as hard as he did, gathering information about enemy troops. They took pictures of shorelines and landmarks to form maps. They intercepted and decoded German messages. One OSS agent was an inventor who created a type of dynamite that looked like baking flour. When kneaded into dough, it became a deadly explosive. Another secret weapon was a broken pencil. It turned out to be a gun with one bullet. Working together, the OSS agents set up "Operation Tropical." Secret agents infiltrated German Intelligence. They tricked the Germans into waiting in one town while American and British troops invaded another town.

After the war, Eisenhower said that a large part of America's victory was due to the Office of Strategic Services, currently known as the CIA (Central Intelligence Agency). William Donovan was promoted to the rank of major general in the army and received many more medals. When he died in 1959, William Donovan was one of the most decorated and remembered war heroes in America.

Drawing Conclusions

1. Why do you think Donovan used actors, photographers, and deep sea divers as undercover agents against the enemy?

   _____

   _____

2. How would an Office of Strategic Services be helpful to a country's war effort? _____

   _____

3. Why wasn't Donovan surprised when the Japanese bombed Pearl Harbor?

   _____

   _____

   _____

Context Clues

4. Donovan *recruited* many people to work as secret agents.
   a. rescued
   b. hired
   c. rewarded

5. The agents worked *undercover* for the OSS.
   a. in secret
   b. underground
   c. with friends

6. The OSS team *infiltrated* the German office.
   a. bombed and killed
   b. was inferior to
   c. attacked and gained control from within

Charge of the Light Brigade

The Crimean War was fought in the 1850s. Turks, French, and British joined forces against the Russians on the peninsula of Crimea in the southern part of the U.S.S.R. During the battle of Balaklava, something went wrong. A troop of about six hundred British horsemen, the Light Brigade, was ordered to attack a strong Russian post. The order was a mistake, but the soldiers obeyed without question. Alfred, Lord Tennyson, told the story of the brave but doomed cavalry in the poem *Charge of the Light Brigade*.

I
Half a league, half a league,
　Half a league onward,
All in the valley of Death
　Rode the six hundred.
"Forward the Light Brigade!
Charge for the guns!" he said:
Into the valley of Death
　Rode the six hundred.

II
"Forward, the Light Brigade!"
Was there a man dismay'd?
Not tho' the soldier knew
　Some one had blunder'd:
Theirs not to make reply,
Theirs not to reason why,
Theirs but to do and die:
Into the valley of Death
　Rode the six hundred.

V
Cannon to right of them,
Cannon to left of them
Cannon behind them
　Volley'd and thunder'd;
Storm'd at with shot and shell,
While horse and hero fell,
They that had fought so well
Came thro' the jaws of Death
Back from the mouth of Hell,
All that was left of them,
　Left of six hundred.

Context Clues

1. When the horsemen *charged*, they
   a. used credit cards to buy horses.
   b. rushed forward.
   c. set off a blast of dynamite.
2. In the poem, *league* is a
   a. part of a horse bridle.
   b. baseball team.
   c. measurement of about three miles.
3. To *blunder* is to _____ .

Inference

4. T　F　Many soldiers were killed in the charge.
5. T　F　The British attack was a success.
6. T　F　The soldiers knew the order was a mistake.

Following Through

7. a. Read the other three stanzas of the poem.
   b. The Crimean War was the first in which women — as nurses — played an important role under Florence Nightingale. Check her life story. Was she fighting disease or wounds? How successful was her nursing?
   c. Yalta, a city on the coast of the Crimea, was the place where a famous World War II meeting was held. Discover what countries took part and why.

Spielberg's Adventures

Among Hollywood filmmakers, the name Steven Spielberg is magic! All of his movies are hits. Part of the magic of his success is the result of Steven's personal involvement with his films. He makes each movie for a different reason. For example, *Jaws* and *Poltergeist* are movies about things that Steven fears. *Close Encounters of the Third Kind* and *E. T.* express Steven's vision of the future. *Raiders of the Lost Ark* and *Indiana Jones and the Temple of Doom* are fun and adventuresome. *Gremlins*, *Back to the Future*, and *Hook* are intended to be pleasing to children. *Jurassic Park*, a record-setting money-maker, was noted for its special effects. And *Schindler's List* is one of Steven's first serious dramas for adults.

Steven began shooting movies when he was a young boy. He wrote scripts, used his family as a cast, and borrowed his father's home movie camera to film his own movies. When he was 13, he won a Boy Scout Photography Merit Badge for a three-minute Western called *The Last Gun*. At 16, Steven shot his first feature length movie, called *Firelight*. Then he rented a movie theater for one evening to show his film. Steven studied at California State College at Long Beach in order to be near Hollywood. He spent hours at Universal Studio's lot where he watched directors and filmmakers in action. All this preparation paid off. By the time he was 30, he had made over six million dollars and several "blockbuster" movies.

The movies Steven directs are action-packed. They are full of special effects and often delight and scare audiences. He works hard to make his movies exciting. Each scene in his films is planned in detail before it is shot. Steven drew 2700 sketches of what he wanted in the movie *Raiders of the Lost Ark* before he even began shooting the film. As a director, Steven must insure that all of the lights, cameras, and special effects props are in the correct position. He also helps the actors understand the script and their roles in it. Steven likes to work with children. It has been said that Spielberg is the best director of children now working in American movies.

After a movie is shot, Spielberg spends a great deal of time editing the film, correcting mistakes or re-shooting scenes, if needed. Steven doesn't consider his movies finished until after an audience has seen a preview. When Spielberg showed a preview of his movie *Jaws*, he noticed that the audience wasn't frightened by a particular scene. With his own money, Steven went back and re-shot the scene, using a mechanical shark in his friend's swimming pool.

continued . . .

11

MP3393

This kind of attention to detail is what makes Steven one of the most exciting filmmakers in Hollywood. Steven is sought after by many of the leading film studios. He has even started his own studio. Plans for new Spielberg movies are always in the making, and each one promises to be different and even more exciting than the last!

Drawing Conclusions

1. What are some characteristics that make a good director? _____
_____
_____
_____

2. Why do you think Steven's films are so popular?_____
_____
_____
_____

Context Clues

3. Steven used his family as a *cast* in the movie.
   a. friend
   b. audience
   c. a set of actors and actresses

4. A *preview* of *Jaws* was shown before it was played at the theater.
   a. seen beforehand
   b. seen afterward
   c. seen at night

5. The film is *edited* by the director.
   a. filmed
   b. directed
   c. put together

Following Through

6. Find out about Steven Spielberg's latest films and the reasons why he produced them.

Can You Solve This Mystery?

Maria Hernandez, 49, was a chemical engineer who worked for a large plastics manufacturer. Her office was on the fifth floor between those of the manager, Mr. Brent, and John, another engineer. The office was just large enough for Maria's necessary things. Against one wall were a filing cabinet and typewriter. On the opposite wall was a bookcase filled with math books and music tapes. Maria's favorite songs were there and she often played them at lunchtime to relax. On the desk were folders, pens, pencils, a telephone, and photographs of Maria's parents. She was their only child. They had been able to give her the best training possible.

The training paid off. One Friday morning, Maria told Mr. Brent that she had created a new formula for making better plastic bottles. Mr. Brent was pleased, and told her she could mix the formula with materials in the plant over the weekend. He promised to tell the watchman to let her into the building.

Early Monday morning, Mr. Brent received a call from a nearby hospital. It was Maria's doctor reporting that she had suffered a stroke on Sunday evening. Although she would get better, at present she could neither move nor speak. Worried about Maria and about her important formula, Mr. Brent hurried to the plant. John was just arriving, and Mr. Brent told him about Maria and the new formula. "I must find that formula. You know the way Maria works. Come and help me find it," he said.

The two men went to Maria's office and began to search. Suddenly the door opened and a young girl walked in. "Good morning," she said. "I'm Inez Hernandez, Maria's niece. I came to get my aunt's tapes so she could listen to her favorites while she gets better." Mr. Brent nodded and the two men continued to look. Inez began to fill a briefcase with the tapes. John shut the last desk drawer just as Inez snapped the briefcase shut. They both started toward the door. "Stop right there," said Mr. Brent. "I know who has the formula."

How did he know?

continued . . .

"I'm Inez Hernandez, Maria's niece. I came to get my aunt's tapes."

13

MP3393

MARIA HERNANDEZ

Inference
1. Maria's new formula would probably
    a. contain water.
    b. make profits for the company.
    c. not work correctly.

Drawing Conclusions
2. Mr. Brent thought the formula was
    a. very important.
    b. in Maria's desk.
    c. at the hospital.

Context Clues
3. A *niece* is a
    a. best friend.
    b. neighbor.
    c. daughter of one's brother or sister.
4. When Maria *created* a new formula she _____ it.
    a. typed
    b. lost
    c. produced

Significant Details
5. Maria was a
    a. railroad engineer.
    b. chemical engineer.
    c. photographer.
6. Maria's formula would make better
    a. plastic bottles.
    b. tapes.
    c. photographs.

Solution:
Mr. Brent became suspicious when Inez said she was Maria's *niece*. As an only child, Maria could not have a niece. He also remembered that another plastics company was looking for a new formula on bottles, too. He suspected Inez had been sent to steal it. He was right. The formula was on a tape and Inez had bribed the watchman to tell her where to find it.

MP3393

Chinese Warriors

Archaeologists, who study early civilizations by digging up items from the past, are like detectives solving mysteries. They look for clues and check evidence. They make deductions and try to find out how ancient people lived. One of the most interesting recent "finds" was made in 1974.

About a mile from a hill that covered an unexplored grave in northwestern China, farmers were digging wells. They did not find water, but they did discover a large underground room. It was filled with handsomely carved, life-size soldiers and horses. When archaeologists from the Chinese Academy of Social Sciences took over, they found a huge army, approximately 6,000, of these pottery soldiers. They also found two teams of four chariot horses, with their harnesses, each drawing a two-wheeled bronze chariot complete with a driver. Some soldiers carry weapons and some walk next to these chariots. The bronze spears and crossbows are still shiny, and traces of bright paint remain on the armor and clothing of the soldiers. This army guards the tomb of Ch'in Shih Huang Ti, China's first emperor.

Ch'in, who ruled from 246 B.C. to 210 B.C., united China and built its Great Wall. Afraid of dying, he spent years having his tomb built. That tomb still lies under its high hill. Within the tomb it is believed that there is a great relief map of the empire, with mercury flowing in the river channels. It was ancient custom to bury a live army with its ruler. The army gave protection from unknown evils in the afterworld. Ch'in decided against actually burying his soldiers, but it is obvious that he had each statue modeled from a different live soldier. When the emperor died at age 49, legend has it that his burial chamber was filled with molten copper so that his coffin was sealed within a huge metal ingot.

Although these figures are unusually fine, they are just the beginning. Old stories tell of wonderful things to be found in Ch'in's actual tomb — gold, jewels, paintings, rich materials, and much more. Although the walls and temples have almost disappeared,

continued . . .

15

MP3393

and many of the artifacts above ground have been stolen, the tomb itself remains relatively undisturbed. It may take hundreds of years for archaeologists to fully realize the magnificence of this 2,000-year-old civilization.

Main Idea

1. The most important event in this story is the discovery of _____.

Inference

2. The people who worked on Ch'in's tomb were probably
   a. good soldiers.
   b. very old.
   c. fine artists.

3. The afterworld is the place where the Chinese believe they live
   a. when they are old.
   b. when they are wealthy.
   c. when they are dead.

Drawing Conclusions

4. Emperor Ch'in was
   a. rich.
   b. cruel.
   c. brave.

Context Clues

5. The *tomb* is the place where
   a. farmers found several figures.
   b. farmers found water.
   c. Ch'in is buried.

6. An *obvious* fact is
   a. well-hidden.
   b. easy to understand or see.
   c. a false statement.

Significant Details

7. What do archaeologists dig up?

   _____

8. Statues of the buried soldiers were made of
   a. iron.
   b. pottery.
   c. bronze.

Following Through

9. Many books have been written about recent Chinese archaeological finds. Read about exhibitions from Chinese tombs and make a list of some of the objects found.

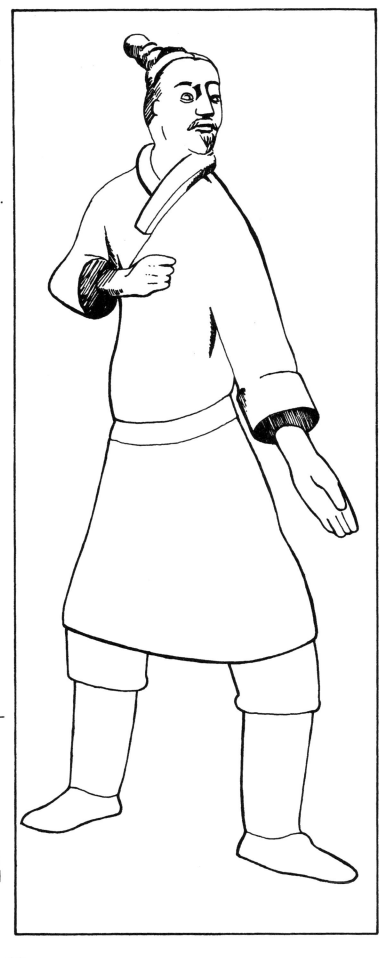

The Hound of the Baskervilles

Sherlock Holmes, the most famous detective of all time, was created by English author Sir Arthur Conan Doyle. One of Holmes' best-known cases is *The Hound of the Baskervilles*. In the story, Holmes and his assistant, Dr. Watson, were called from London to Baskerville Hall to investigate a murder. There was a very frightening clue. Near the body of the murdered man were the footprints of a giant hound. Holmes learned of a Baskerville family legend about a ghostlike dog that ran the moors. Although Holmes heard howling in the night, it was almost the end of the story before he saw the dog.

One night, Holmes, Dr. Watson, and a police inspector hid close to a path that the murderous hound might take. From various clues, Holmes had deduced when the animal would strike. The path leading from the Hall to Grimpen Mire, a quicksand on the moor, was covered with fog. It was a perfect night for a ghost to walk. Holmes almost missed seeing Sir Henry Baskerville as he came down the path on his nightly walk. Sir Henry, Holmes guessed, would be the next murder victim. In a few minutes,

continued . . .

the sound of crisp, continuous patter came through the fog. Holmes pulled out his gun. The others waited fearfully. Would it be the hound? Could it be stopped by bullets?

Suddenly a huge, black shape bounded through the fog. It was a coal-black hound the size of a female lion. Holmes and Watson stared in wonder. Never had they seen such a savage creature. Fire seemed to burst from its open mouth. Its eyes glowed. Its muzzle and jaws were outlined in flickering flame. Taking large bounds, the huge black creature leaped after Sir Henry.

Holmes, Watson, and the Inspector recovered from their shock and raced after the creature. They saw it spring at Sir Henry's throat and pull him to the ground. Holmes fired five shots into the animal's side. With a last howl and a vicious snap in the air, it rolled on its back. Its feet pawed furiously, and it fell limp. The giant hound was dead. Sir Henry was saved from certain death.

Main Idea
1. The most important person in this story is
   a. the black hound.
   b. Sherlock Holmes.
   c. Sir Henry.

Inference
2. T F The hound was a ghost.
3. T F The hound was small.
4. T F The hound frightened people.

Significant Details
5. When Holmes saw the hound, he pulled out a _____ .

Context Clues
6. When the detective *deduced* the answer to the mystery, he
   a. wrote it.
   b. read it.
   c. figured it out.
7. *Continuous* means _____ .

Drawing Conclusions
8. What kind of detective do you think Holmes was?
   a. successful
   b. frightened
   c. stupid

Following Through
9. Read the entire story of *The Hound of the Baskervilles.*
10. Another fictional detective, Nero Wolfe, has an assistant. Read one of his mysteries, written by Rex Stout. How much help does Holmes' assistant give him? _____

   _____

   How much does Nero's assistant give?

   _____

   _____

   Which detective does the most work?

   _____

Tiger Woods

Before Eldrick Woods reached his first birthday, he knew how to swing a golf club. Eldrick, nicknamed "Tiger" after his dad's courageous war buddy, just naturally took to the game. Tiger's parents often let their young son practice his golf swing at the nearby Navy Golf Course. They knew that their son was unusual. Most toddlers were busy mastering the basics of walking and talking, but Tiger was mastering his golf shots. When he was just two years old, Tiger was featured on local television. When he was five, he appeared on a popular TV show, *That's Incredible!*, because it was very unusual for a five-year-old to be so talented.

Both of Tiger's parents wanted him to have a strong character. They insisted on good grades and good sportsmanship. Tiger remembered these lessons throughout his life. He played many sports in high school, but eventually gave them all up for golf. By the time he was 14, Tiger had won five world titles, more than any other golfer his age had ever won. While in high school, Tiger won the United States Junior Amateur Championship three times. Many colleges wanted this young golf star on their team. Tiger finally decided to attend Stanford University on a full golf scholarship.

Tiger studied economics in college and worked hard. He played golf on the college team and ventured out into some PGA tournaments with more experienced players. Tiger studied these players and their techniques, and incorporated their methods into his own. A personal goal was met when Tiger won the National Collegiate Athlete Association (NCAA) golf championship.

Tiger had won many titles and champion-ships, but only as an amateur. The true test was to play against professional golfers. Many critics thought Tiger was too young to turn pro. But

Tiger felt he was ready. He had met all the challenges as an amateur and was prepared to move on.

Tiger started well on the professional circuit. Older, more experienced golfers were impressed with his talents. More importantly, however, they were impressed wih his composure and sportsman-like qualities. Tiger never got angry or lost his temper, even if he shot an easy putt into

the sand trap. His parents had taught him the importance of upstanding conduct, and he wouldn't let them down. Tiger went on to win title after title. He would often worry his fans with a slow start, but would delight them with a strong finish. Tiger valued the fans that followed him from tournament to tournament. Every day there seemed to be more young people in the crowds.

continued . . .

Tiger was pleased about that. He was making a contribution to the game of golf by introducing it to many new, young players. Together, he and his dad help young people by providing golf clinics. Some youngsters would never have been exposed to a golf course if it weren't for Tiger.

Tiger's great golf game promises to continue. He also continues to deserve the title he received in 1996 —"Sportsman of the Year." Tiger has skill and unusual talent combined with a spirit of responsibility and fair play. This winning combination makes him a true "sportsman."

Main Idea
1. Tiger Woods excels at
   a. sports.
   b. college.
   c. golf.

Significant Details
2. Tiger began swinging a club
   a. as a toddler.
   b. when he was five.
   c. in high school.
3. In college, Tiger won the
   a. NCAA championship.
   b. Sportsman of the Year Award.
   c. golf scholarship.

Context Clues
4. Golf pros were impressed with Tiger's *composure*.
   a. golf swing
   b. ability to stay calm
   c. young age

Inference
5. If Tiger found out that his opponent had cheated on his score, Tiger would probably
   a. call the officials and have the scores changed.
   b. attack his opponent and let everyone know about the cheating.
   c. wait until after the game and confront his opponent quietly.

Drawing Conclusions
6. Tiger's parents never had to push Tiger to practice. Why not?
   a. The game came naturally to Tiger, and he loved playing it.
   b. He was no good at other sports and had to play golf.
   c. His parents don't believe in making a child do something he doesn't want to do.

Andrea in Danger

As usual, by 3:30 everything was quiet in the school library. Andrea sat down at a table and began to work on her report. After a while, she noticed that the room had grown darker. It was not even four o'clock and the sky was black! A loud clap of thunder shook everything in the library! In the stillness that followed, a blast came from the library's computer terminal. Ribbons of green light swirled across the main screen. Even ten feet away Andrea could read: YOU ARE IN DANGER. DO NOT PANIC. PRESS 0 KEY FOR FURTHER INSTRUCTIONS. FOLLOW INSTRUCTIONS EXACTLY OR DISASTER WILL OCCUR IMMEDIATELY.

Finish the story. If necessary, continue on another piece of paper.

America's Detective

When Allan Pinkerton was a young boy, he never dreamed he would become one of America's most respected detectives. In fact, Allan, who was born in Scotland in 1819, had not thought about a career at all. Then his father, a sergeant with the Glasgow police force, was injured while on duty. The father could no longer work, so the Pinkerton boys had to support the family. Allan took a job as a barrelmaker.

When Allan grew up and married, he and his wife moved to America. They settled in a town outside of Chicago, and Allan opened a barrel-making shop. While he was out collecting material for his barrels, Allan began his detective career. He stumbled across evidence of counterfeiting and soon rounded up a gang of counterfeiters which had been secretly working in the Chicago area. Allan became a local hero, and the Chicago police offered him a job as a special investigator.

Pinkerton became very skilled at tracking criminals. He used disguises, reasoning, psychology, and even tricks to catch criminals all over the country. Outlaws feared him the most. They had heard about the way he captured the Reno brothers, a Wild West gang of about 100 men. They also knew he had broken up the Molly Maguires, a group that tried to destroy the coal-mining industry.

By this time, Allan had set up the Pinkerton National Detective Agency, with branch offices in many cities. All across the country, his specially trained agents were tracking down criminals and other lawbreakers. Today, Pinkerton's Agency is one of the largest investigative and security agencies in the world. Over 13,000 employees work in 48 cities in the United States and Canada. And Allan Pinkerton, who died in 1884, is still called America's first great detective.

Main Idea
1. The Pinkerton Agency developed as a result of Allan Pinkerton's
   a. counterfeiting.
   b. investigating.
   c. studying.

Significant Details
2. Pinkerton became a detective
   a. by accident.
   b. after years of study.
   c. after he fell down.
3. The Pinkerton Agency operates in
   a. Scotland.
   b. Europe.
   c. North America.

Inference
4. Allan Pinkerton may have inherited some of his crime-solving skills from
   a. the Chicago police.
   b. his father.
   c. his strict Scottish upbringing.

Drawing Conclusions
5. Pinkerton died a wealthy man. Why would you assume this is true?
   a. Counterfeiters gave him a great deal of money to keep their secret.
   b. He sold his barrel-making business for a huge profit.
   c. The Pinkerton Agency has been large and successful for a long time.

The Golden Gate Bridge

Half a century ago many people said it couldn't be built. But in 1987, thousands of people celebrated the fiftieth anniversary of the opening of San Francisco's Golden Gate Bridge.

The Golden Gate itself was formed by nature. It is a deep channel at the entrance to San Francisco Bay. It measures four miles long and about a mile wide. It is deep enough for even the largest ships to travel through.

The Gate's history goes back a long way. An English explorer, Sir Francis Drake, saw it in 1578. But it is believed that John C. Fremont, an American explorer, named it the Golden Gate. In 1849, people on their way to look for gold thought the name was good luck. And so the name has remained.

In the early 1900s, anyone traveling north from San Francisco had two choices. They could take a ferry across the "Gate," or make a long detour to the south. People began wondering if a bridge could be built to cross over the four-mile gap. In 1923, a group was formed to study the problem. Many members of the group did not think a bridge was possible. But Joseph Strauss, an engineer, said he could design and build a bridge. There were many problems and delays. But at last Strauss finished the Golden Gate Bridge, one of the largest suspension bridges in the world.

Californians were proud of their new bridge, which was finished on May 26, 1937. The next day was "Pedestrian Day." From 6:00 a.m. to 6:00 p.m. almost 200,000 people walked or ran or danced across the six lanes of this wonderful new bridge. Late in the afternoon, one of the visitors called for quiet. "Listen to the bridge," he said. High up among the suspension wires, the wind was shrieking. From below came the deep roar of the water as it struck the piers. The bridge was like a giant wind harp. Fifty years later, the Golden Gate Bridge is still playing its song.

Main Idea
1. This story tells about a
   a. difficult building project.
   b. group of gold-seekers.
   c. band of explorers.

Significant Details
2. The Golden Gate Bridge is
   a. near New York City.
   b. on the Mississippi River.
   c. near San Francisco Bay.
3. When was the bridge built?
   a. over fifty years ago
   b. in early 1500s
   c. during the gold rush

Context Clues
4. A *pedestrian* is someone who
   a. builds bridges.
   b. climbs mountains.
   c. goes on foot.

Drawing Conclusions
5. Do you think the bridge was built properly?
   a. Yes, it is still there after more than fifty years.
   b. Yes, it does not sway at all.
   c. No, the fog makes the end of the bridge hard to see.

Floating Markets

Shopping in Bangkok, Thailand is a real treat. Instead of rushing through crowded malls and narrow grocery aisles, shoppers in Bangkok have their merchandise brought to them.

Buying from floating markets is the way to shop in Bangkok. Each day local merchants pile their goods in flatboats called sampans. They sail down Bangkok's many canals, selling their wares. The brimming sampans make a colorful sight with their baskets of melons, coconuts, and other exotic fruits grown in Thailand.

Some shoppers sail out to meet the sampans. Others just lean over from the shore to make their purchases. Some sampans are equipped with small stoves and can offer hot meals to customers.

Almost anything can be bought from the floating markets. Fresh fruits, vegetables, spices, charcoal, and even medicines are sold on sampans. Some of the newer sampans carry clothing and souvenirs for tourists. The canals are noisy places because each merchant calls out what he has to sell.

Eighty years ago there was only one road in Bangkok. People traveled everywhere by boat. The floating markets proved to be an easy way to shop. For a person who had no refrigerator, shopping at a floating market provided fresh food for each meal. Times have changed in Bangkok. Many new roads have been built and living conditions have greatly improved. But the floating markets still provide a special, enjoyable way to shop.

Main Idea
1. People in Bangkok use their canals
   a. to beat the traffic on the crowded highways.
   b. for buying and selling products.
   c. for swimming and recreation.

Significant Details
2. Sampans are
   a. exotic fruits.
   b. local merchants.
   c. boats with flat bottoms.
3. Shoppers can choose their groceries
   a. from bright display shelves.
   b. while standing on the shore.
   c. from the roads of Bangkok.

Context Clues
4. The merchants sold their *wares*.
   a. goods
   b. sampans
   c. motorboats

Inference
5. Boat-building might be a good business in Bangkok because
   a. the people there have never seen modern motorboats.
   b. the people there are wealthy and could buy many boats.
   c. boating is a daily means of travel in Bangkok.

Drawing Conclusions
6. With new roads and modern conveniences, why would people in Bangkok still use floating markets?
   a. The markets provide an easy and cheap way to shop.
   b. Bangkok hasn't built any grocery stores yet.
   c. The markets are the only place to get fresh fish.

Moving a Monument

The Nile River is often called the "lifeline" of Egypt. It has long been a means of transportation for Egyptians and a source of irrigation for their farm lands. But it has also caused some problems. Each year, after heavy spring rains, the Nile floods.

To control the summer floods, a huge dam, the Aswan High Dam, was suggested. One thing stood in the way. The huge lake which would form behind the dam would completely cover an important ancient temple with water.

The temple was built on the banks of the Nile by Rameses II, a powerful Pharaoh of early Egypt, to honor Egyptian gods. The inside halls of this monument were cut into the sandstone mountain. Across the front were four gigantic stone figures of Rameses, each 65 feet tall.

An Egyptian sculptor thought of a way to save the temple. People from all over the world gave money so that this monument could be moved out of the path of the new lake. The stone temple was sawed into thousands of blocks. Each block was numbered and then lifted by crane from its original place. The blocks were put back together several hundred yards away. It took 2000 workers and almost seven years to put the blocks back together. Now the dam is finished, the lake is deep, and the four giants are safe and dry in their new home.

Main Idea
1. This story is mainly about
   a. the life and times of ancient Egypt.
   b. saving an important work of art.
   c. the four battles of Rameses II.

Significant Details
2. What did engineers plan to build on the Nile River?
   a. a temple
   b. a statue
   c. a dam
3. How long did it take to rebuild the monument?
   a. nearly a year
   b. 7 years
   c. 7 months
4. Why is the Nile called Egypt's lifeline?
   a. Egyptians use it for transportation and irrigation.
   b. Many Egyptians are born there.
   c. It is the home of the gods.

Context Clues
5. *Irrigation* for crops
   a. provides water so they can grow.
   b. keeps weeds from choking plants.
   c. is a new method of night gardening.
6. Rameses was a *Pharaoh* of early Egypt.
   a. god
   b. worker
   c. king

Drawing Conclusions
7. People from all over the world want to save historic treasures. How can you tell this is true?
   a. They allowed the temple to be sawed into pieces.
   b. They gave money so that a temple could be saved.
   c. They like to ride on the Nile River.

This Pharaoh Was a Woman

Hatshepsut was one of the most famous women in ancient Egypt. She was the daughter of a Pharaoh, the wife of another, and the aunt of a third. When Hatshepsut's father died, her husband succeeded him as Pharaoh, and she became Queen of Egypt. After a short time, her husband died, which left a nephew to succeed to the throne. Hatshepsut refused to accept her nephew as Pharaoh.

Hatshepsut said the boy was not of royal blood. She argued that *she* was the rightful ruler. Hatshepsut did not want to give up control of the country to a boy. So she sent her nephew away to study with Egyptian priests and seized the throne herself. Even though all the past Pharaohs had been men, Hatshepsut declared herself the new Pharaoh.

To make sure that the Egyptians would accept her as ruler, Hatshepsut dressed in her husband's tunic with its lion tail down the back. She also carried the royal scepter and wore the high double crown of Egypt.

Hatshepsut's father had been a warrior Pharaoh. He captured many tribes and extended the boundaries of Egypt. But Hatshepsut did not want to wage wars. Instead, she hoped to extend her country's boundaries by trading. Under her rule, Egypt had a peaceful and prosperous time, the best for many years. Hatshepsut also built many temples and monuments. Some of these beautiful buildings remain today as a tribute to Egypt's only woman Pharaoh.

Main Idea
1. The most important person in this story
   a. is a young nephew.
   b. is an Egyptian ruler.
   c. is the warrior Pharaoh.

Significant Details
2. Hatshepsut's crown was
   a. made entirely of gold.
   b. covered with lions' tails.
   c. the high double crown of Egypt.
3. Hatshepsut's father was a
   a. warrior Pharaoh.
   b. weak ruler.
   c. famous sailor.

Context Clues
4. A *tunic* is a
   a. piece of music.
   b. hat.
   c. piece of clothing like a long shirt.

5. Egypt was *prosperous*.
   a. poor
   b. wealthy and successful
   c. at war

Inference
6. How can you tell that Hatshepsut cared about her country?
   a. She worked to keep it peaceful and prosperous.
   b. She sent her nephew off to study.
   c. She spent her time planning wars for Egypt.

Drawing Conclusions
7. Was Hatshepsut a strong-willed woman?
   a. Yes, she insisted on marrying a Pharaoh.
   b. No, she did not like fighting.
   c. Yes, she took the throne away from her nephew.

Twenty-four Hours in Le Mans

The first Grand Prix auto race was held in Le Mans, France, in 1906. It seemed only natural that a new type of auto racing, an endurance race, would also have its start there.

Grand Prix racing was becoming very strict. Exact rules required each car to meet certain standards before it was allowed to enter the race. But the average spectator was not really interested in the way in which a racing engine was built. Racing fans wanted to see an exciting race. Since few cars were allowed to take part in the race, many people began to lose interest in the race.

Two men in Le Mans, Charles Faroux and George Durant, decided to change the rules so more cars could enter the race. They planned a new race for which the cars had to meet only three simple conditions. The contest was to last twenty-four hours. The winner of the race would be the car that traveled the greatest distance in the 24-hour time period. This made it a true test of endurance. People in Le Mans were delighted by this new race that would follow the real roads through their city. European car makers rushed to enter their latest autos.

Over the years, there have been many rule changes. One year the drivers actually had to drive part of the race with their hoods up! Luckily, race fans were willing to settle for some less dangerous changes. Because of the new dangers caused by high speeds, road circuits have been moved from busy cities and towns. An 8.36 mile road circuit was laid out for the race just south of the city of Le Mans. A few more rules were added to the qualifying list. But basically the Le Mans 24-hour Grand Prix, the world's best known automobile race, has remained what it was first meant to be — a contest of strength and endurance.

Mercedes-Benz
1906 at Le Mans, France

Main Idea
1. The most popular race in Le Mans is
   a. the 24-hour endurance run.
   b. the French Grand Prix.
   c. the European stock car race.

Significant Details
2. A new type of racing developed because
   a. Grand Prix racing was too dangerous.
   b. The town of Le Mans wanted to attract visitors.
   c. People were losing interest in the Grand Prix.
3. The Le Mans Grand Prix is run
   a. on a road circuit outside Le Mans.
   b. on an indoor track.
   c. on an outdoor track.

Context Clues
4. *Spectators* lost interest in the sport.
   a. race car drivers
   b. people who watch an event
   c. people who design car engines
5. In this story, a *circuit* means
   a. an electric element.
   b. the strict rules.
   c. the route traveled.

Drawing Conclusions
6. Do people today basically agree with Faroux and Durant's ideas?
   a. No, the race has been canceled.
   b. No, the idea of endurance racing did not last.
   c. Yes, only a few changes in the original race idea have been made.

Mark McGwire

It was 10-year-old Mark McGwire's very first official Little League baseball game. He stepped up to bat, waited for his first pitch, and hit his first official home run. Anyone watching that Little League game knew that young Mark was off to a great start in baseball. His father said Mark understood the game of baseball at an early age. Mark was interested in being a pitcher, but at the same time was racking up home runs. By the time he played for his high school team, his pitching and home-run hitting caught the attention of a sports scout from the University of Southern California. The scout offered Mark a full scholarship to college if he would play as a pitcher on their team. At the same time, however, another tempting offer came Mark's way. The Montreal Expos offered him a position on their team as soon as he graduated from high school. It was a hard decision, but Mark wisely chose to attend college first.

He had a great college baseball career at USC, where he began setting records for home-run hitting. It was during college when his pitching focus changed. Mark spent an off-season summer playing for the Anchorage Glacier Pilots. The team positioned him at first base, and Mark found that he played well there. Slowly, he gave up pitching and concentrated on hitting.

Those hits got him noticed. It wasn't long before he was playing major league ball with the Oakland A's. His first year with the team was exciting for Mark. He was named American League Rookie of the Year, and that same year his son, Matthew, was born.

Mark was a good athlete and played in the World Series three times within his first four seasons. But he was ready for a change. He switched leagues in mid-season and joined the St. Louis Cardinals. When Mark came to St. Louis, he had already scored 34 runs. Another 24 runs as a Cardinal gave him a total of 58 runs in one season. Mark was very close to breaking a long-standing record.

Thirty-seven years before, player Roger Maris set a home-run record of 61 home runs in one season. No one had come near the record since then. Could Mark McGwire beat it? St. Louis Cardinal fans thought he could. Thousands came to see Mark McGwire play, and they weren't disappointed. As if he knew the fans were waiting, McGwire stepped up to the plate on opening day of the 1998 season and thrilled the crowds with a grand-slam home run. The race was on! Could this be the year Roger Maris's record was broken? Fans across the country began to keep track of McGwire's home runs. By the end of April, Mark had homered 11 times. In August, Mark scored his 50th home run. At the same time, Sammy Sosa of the Chicago Cubs was hitting just as many. Would one of these two ballplayers hit the record number before the season was over?

continued . . .

28

MP3393

On September 7, Mark McGwire did it. He hit his 61st home run to tie the old Roger Maris record. The fans went wild with excitement. They knew that they had just witnessed history being made. But the next night was even better. It was the Cardinal's last game in St. Louis, and to make it even more exciting, the visiting team was Sammy Sosa's Chicago Cubs. Would this be the night the record was finally broken? Fans didn't have long to wait. Mark McGwire stepped up to the plate, swung, and sent the ball sailing over the fence. Home run #62! He had done it! Again, the fans were on their feet, screaming and cheering. Busch Stadium lit up like the Fourth of July. But Mark didn't notice. He was too busy hugging his son, Matthew, and shaking hands with the children of Roger Maris. He was also being hugged by his good friend and rival, Sammy Sosa.

It was hard to settle down after that explosive game, but the season continued, and McGwire ended it with a total of 70 home runs. Mark had come a long way from his first home run in Little League.

Main Idea

1. Mark McGwire is best known for his
   a. pitching ability.
   b. hitting ability.
   c. kicking ability.

Significant Details

2. Mark played one summer season with the
   a. Anchorage Glacier Pilots.
   b. St. Louis Cardinals.
   c. Chicago Cubs.

3. During Mark's first year in the major league, he
   a. broke the home-run record.
   b. was named Rookie of the Year.
   c. hit 58 home runs.

Context Clues

4. The crowd had just *witnessed* history being made.
   a. seen
   b. participated in
   c. enjoyed

Inference

5. Family is important to Mark. How do you know that?
   a. He moved his family to St. Louis.
   b. His father came to every game.
   c. He shared his victory with his son first.

Drawing Conclusions

6. Good athletes often set goals. If Mark McGwire were a goal setter, what goals do you think he would set for himself?

   _____
   _____
   _____
   _____

Beethoven

Most classical music concerts in the last 100 years have included a symphony or concerto by Beethoven. Why is this man's music so often chosen? Why do people want to hear his work over and over? It may be because Beethoven has written one of the most powerful collections of music ever put together by one composer.

Ludwig van Beethoven was born in Bonn, Germany, in 1770. His father and grandfather were both musicians, so Beethoven himself turned to music. Before Ludwig's time, composers wrote works for religious services, teaching, and entertainment at social functions. But people listened to Beethoven's music for its own sake.

Ludwig began studying music at a very young age. He played the piano, violin, and organ. From the beginning he was a creator. He was full of ideas, originality, and power. His sketchbooks show that he revised his works many times. It often took years of rewriting before he was satisfied with the whole piece.

When he was a young man, Beethoven moved to Vienna, Austria, the center of the music world at that time. There he enjoyed much success. Many of the great composers of the day, including Haydn and Mozart,

were hired by wealthy people to write music and play for them. Beethoven was also paid money for his works. But he demanded to be treated as a friend and an equal by royalty and the wealthy.

Later in life, tragedy struck. Beethoven realized he was going deaf. What could be worse than a musician who could not hear? Although the increasing deafness made Beethoven's work difficult, he did not stop. In fact, he moved into a more interesting style of composing. By the end of his life, Beethoven was composing, playing, and conducting music that he could hear only inside his head. And that music, created by a bold, determined artist, has never been surpassed.

Main Idea
1. This story is mainly about a
    a. trip to Vienna.
    b. happy music teacher.
    c. musical genius.

Significant Details
2. Beethoven was born in the city of
    a. Vienna.
    b. Paris.
    c. Bonn.
3. Beethoven played the piano and
    a. the flute.
    b. the violin.
    c. the drums.

Context Clues
4. Beethoven had a lot of *originality*.
    a. new ideas
    b. wealth
    c. sketchbooks

Drawing Conclusions
5. What was unusual about the last music Beethoven conducted?
    a. It was the longest ever played.
    b. He could not hear how it sounded.
    c. He received no pay for it.
6. Beethoven did not want
    a. to be paid for his music.
    b. to ever change a note of his music.
    c. to be treated like hired help.

Scientific Glassblower

Jim Franklin has an unusual job. He is one of a very few people who specialize in scientific glassblowing. The ancient art of glassblowing began in the Near East during the first century, B.C. By blowing molten glass through a hollow tube, bubbles of glass can be shaped into beautiful objects.

In 1898, the first automatic glassblowing machine was introduced. This reduced the need for human glassblowers. Huge numbers of glassware were made in pre-set molds.

But scientists found that their glass needs could not be met by molds. Each new research project needed glass equipment with a new shape or design. Because of this, scientific glassblowing became a highly specialized field.

New Jersey has the only glassblowing school in the country. Therefore, most scientific glassblowers learn their trade from experienced craftsmen on the job. Jim had to learn his job in a hurry. He was working for Washington University in St. Louis, Missouri, when the head glassblower retired. Jim was to take his place and had only three months to learn the skills. Jim has mastered the techniques. But because each project requires a new piece of glass, he is still adding to his skills as he works.

Scientists come to Jim with rough drawings of what they want. Working with rods and tubes, Jim shapes, bends, expands, and heats the glass until a complex piece of glassware is produced. Without Jim Franklin and the glassware he makes, scientists would not be able to conduct many of their research projects.

Main Idea
1. Jim's work
   a. helps scientists with research.
   b. can be done with molds.
   c. is no longer needed.

Significant Details
2. Jim constantly learns new techniques on the job because
   a. glassblowing is hard to learn.
   b. Washington University does not teach glassblowing.
   c. each project requires him to make a new product.
3. Most scientific glassblowers learn their trade
   a. at Washington University.
   b. in New Jersey.
   c. from master craftsmen.

Context Clues
4. Jim makes *complex* equipment.
   a. complete
   b. complicated
   c. controlled
5. *Molten* glass is
   a. spoiled.
   b. liquid.
   c. hard.

Inference
6. In Jim's work, he might design
   a. a glass tray for baking silicon micro-chips.
   b. wine goblets and other beautiful objects.
   c. a glass door which would lock from the inside.

MP3393

The Knighthood of Roland

(Adapted from a French medieval tale)

More than anything else, young Roland wanted to become a knight. He looked forward to wearing shining armor, carrying a silver sword, and fighting for justice. But for now, Roland was just a squire, a boy in training for knighthood. Roland's uncle, the good King Charlemagne of France, allowed a group of squires to ride with him on a trip to Italy. Roland and his friend Ogier were proud to be among those who were going with the king. As squires, they were not allowed to wear armor or carry weapons, but they would get to see their favorite knights in action.

King Charlemagne stopped his army at the top of the Alps, the mountain range that separates France from Italy. The enemy was below. Charlemagne decided to send his first division down to surprise the enemy. The rest of his troops would then follow and conquer the evil enemy.

A young knight, Alory, asked to be in the first division. He had been born in France and thought he should be one of the first to save his native country. Charlemagne agreed and watched as Alory led the first division into battle. But something went wrong. The enemy charged from the base of the mountain and attacked the French troops. Alory was so frightened that he turned his horse and fled up the mountain. Many of his friends followed. Angrily, King Charlemagne and the rest of his troops charged down the hill. But it was too late. The enemy was ready for them. They took the King and all his knights as prisoners.

Roland and Ogier were very upset when they saw their King taken prisoner. Quickly they gathered the other squires to join the fight. Most of the squires refused because they knew it was against the rules. But Roland and Ogier were already pulling the

continued . . .

MP3393

cowardly Alory from his horse and taking his sword and shield. The other cowards who had followed Alory gave their weapons to the rest of the squires.

The young boys, now armed like knights, rode down the hill. The enemy thought all the knights had been captured and had already put down their weapons. They were not prepared to fight. After a short battle, the surprised enemy ran in fear, and King Charlemagne was saved. The King was so proud of his young squires that he held a ceremony right on the battlefield. He made Roland and Ogier knights of his court. The two boys were now looked upon as young men. They solemnly took the pledge of knighthood and promised to be truthful, loyal, and fair to all men.

Main Idea

1. In this story, Roland
   a. became King of France.
   b. helped a coward.
   c. proved his bravery.

Significant Details

2. A squire
   a. trains to become a knight.
   b. is not very brave.
   c. fights with shields and swords.

3. The battle with the enemy was almost lost by
   a. Roland.
   b. Alory.
   c. Ogier.

Context Clues

4. A *prisoner* has been
   a. taken by the enemy.
   b. knighted.
   c. killed.

5. In this story, a *coward* is
   a. a young person.
   b. a person who fights well.
   c. someone without courage.

6. They *conquered* the enemy.
   a. defeated
   b. joined
   c. frightened

Inference

7. Which of the following is most important in becoming a knight?
   a. He must be tall and strong.
   b. He must be brave.
   c. He must be an adult.

Drawing Conclusions

8. Do you think Roland was ready to become a knight?
   a. Yes, he had trained as a squire long enough.
   b. Yes, he showed quick thinking and courage.
   c. No, he was still a young boy.

Following Through

9. Find a book about Roland. "The Song of Roland" is the story of his life. Read about the adventures Sir Roland had as a knight. Compare him with young men today.

Vincent van Gogh

Vincent van Gogh had a very short career as an artist. During his lifetime he sold only half-a-dozen canvases. Yet today his work is prized and valuable and he is considered one of the most outstanding painters in modern art.

Van Gogh was born in Holland in 1853. Vincent was a preacher's son and wanted to follow in his father's footsteps. When he tried to enter school to study religion in 1878, he was turned down. It was felt that, with his strange appearance, he did not look like a man of God. Disappointed, he went to work for an art gallery in The Hague, the Dutch capital. Vincent did so well that he was promoted to the London office. He seemed to have found success at last. But when the woman he loved rejected him, Vincent was broken-hearted. She had laughed at him! Troubled and unhappy, Vincent left the art gallery and began preaching in the slums.

He could not forget the young woman and tried again to win her love. She refused him again. He left London and joined a religious mission in Belgium. He worked in a poor, coal-mining area, teaching children and helping the sick. Van Gogh began to draw during this time. He drew the miners and the peasants and tried to picture the hardships of their daily lives. When the mission discovered that he was going without proper food and clothing in order to give more to the poor, they asked him to leave. He had become an embarrassment to them.

Rejected again, Vincent decided to spend all his time painting. His own unhappiness and his concern for the poor can be easily seen in his early paintings. There is a real sadness in them. He used dark, depressing colors and thick, angry brush strokes.

In 1886, Vincent moved to Paris to join his brother, Theo. Paris was the center of the art world and Vincent met many leading artists there. Their Impressionist style of art attracted him immediately. The artists recognized Van Gogh's genius and worked with him. Impressionism is a style of art that features bright, shimmering colors and scenes of life and nature. Vincent learned much about this style, and gradually his own style changed. His brush strokes became lighter and his pictures blazed with color.

Vincent now saw beauty in the world around him and, he longed to put what he saw on canvas. He left the city and moved to Arles, in the South of France. While there, he produced his greatest paintings. He painted hundreds of pictures between 1888 and 1890. He worked quickly, often creating a work of art in a single sitting! Van Gogh expressed his feeling about a subject with color, as in his *Sunflowers*. But in addition to color, Van Gogh also saw movement in nature. In his *Wheat Field and Cypress Trees*, the sky and the earth seem to be moving. The clouds and hills seem ready to move off the canvas, and the wheat field looks like a stormy sea.

continued . . .

During this period, when Van Gogh created his most original and expressive pictures, he suffered fits of mental illness. Violent seizures and his fear of being permanently mad made painting very difficult for him. The slashing brush strokes and intense splashes of color in his last works suggest that he was disturbed. His picture *The Night Cafe* is a good example. He felt that his mental illness could never be cured, and he knew that it would keep him from painting. He committed suicide in 1890, because he felt that only art had made his life worth living.

Van Gogh thought of himself as a failure. He longed to be loved and respected. Without knowing it, he had achieved both. His works of art are admired and desired by people all over the world. Today there is a museum in Amsterdam which is filled with his paintings only. Recently, one of his famous *Sunflowers* paintings was sold for $39.9 million, one of the highest prices ever paid for a single work of art!

Main Idea
1. Van Gogh's paintings can be recognized by
   a. the lovely picture frames.
   b. the bold colors and brush strokes.
   c. the pale watercolors.

Significant Details
2. Van Gogh's first paintings were
   a. bright and happy.
   b. of his father.
   c. dark and sad.
3. Van Gogh got new ideas from
   a. the slums.
   b. artists in France.
   c. his brother, Theo.
4. His ____ recently sold for $39.9 million.
   a. *Sunflowers*
   b. *The Night Cafe*
   c. *Wheat Field and Cypress Trees*

Context Clues
5. The young woman *rejected* him.
   a. turned down
   b. accepted
   c. hired
6. He pictured the *hardships* of their lives.
   a. boats
   b. comforts
   c. suffering
7. Van Gogh *committed suicide*.
   a. killed a friend
   b. took his own life
   c. stole some money

Inference
8. Vincent van Gogh was __ when he died.
   a. 37
   b. 53
   c. 90

Following Through
9. Find out why van Gogh cut off his ear.
10. Find color reproductions of the paintings mentioned in this article. Study them.

Faster Than a Speeding Bullet

Gone are the days when heavy locomotives lumbered along the railroad tracks, puffing out billows of steam. The new era of technology in transportation has developed some of the fastest trains to come along the tracks.

Many countries are developing trains that will increase speed and decrease travel time. These trains would make transportation easier and less expensive. Some countries have already put their trains to work.

The world's fastest electric train is France's high-speed train, the TGV. It runs between Paris and Lyon at an average speed of more than 170 miles (270 kilometers) per hour.

Japanese travelers are speeding to work on a streamlined "bullet train," the Shinkansen. The "bullet train" is one of the fastest in operation. It travels as fast as 130 miles per hour. It operates on elevated tracks that run throughout Tokyo. A third rail sends electric power to the elevated train. The train's engineer controls the flow of current to the train.

Italy is testing its new "tilting train." This high-speed train, the Pendolino, actually tilts at every curve. Developers at first found it difficult to get the train to lean at the right time. The use of gyroscopes solved that problem. By leaning in on a curve, the train gains speed. With this additional speed, a five-hour trip is cut back to four hours.

Germany is trying out the latest development in transportation, magnetic levitation technology. Maglev, as it is called, creates a magnetic field between magnets in the train and the steel in the tracks. A negative force between the magnets and the steel pushes the train up just a fraction of an inch off the track. This allows the "flying train" to fly along the tracks without friction or vibration. The train now carries 260 passengers. Designers believe it will reach speeds up to 250 miles per hour. These trains will be lighter than traditional ones and less expensive to build.

continued . . .

MP3393

All of these trains are quieter than the old locomotives. They do not produce smoke or exhaust. The older locomotives ran only on diesel fuel. These new trains are able to run without gasoline and oil. With all these high-speed developments, it will be interesting to see what next comes down the track.

Main Idea
1. There have been many new developments in the field of
   a. gyroscopes.
   b. transportation.
   c. economy.

Significant Details
2. Italy's train
   a. operates on elevated tracks.
   b. uses negative magnetic forces.
   c. leans as it passes curves.
3. Which train is less expensive to build?
   a. the "bullet train"
   b. the "tilting train"
   c. the "flying train"
4. The TGV train runs in
   a. France.
   b. Italy.
   c. Germany.

Context Clues
5. *Elevated* tracks run
   a. above the ground.
   b. below the ground.
   c. through tunnels.

Inference
6. Airlines may not be pleased with the latest developments because
   a. the technology does not include developments in jets.
   b. airlines don't care about trains.
   c. people may find it better to travel by train.

Drawing Conclusions
7. Germany's "flying train"
   a. is built with a jet engine.
   b. travels above the ground.
   c. can go faster than a jet.
8. Which is true of these new trains?
   a. They cut down noise and air pollution and conserve gas and oil.
   b. They are all underground.
   c. They are all operating in Europe.

Following Through
9. Find out how the TGV, the high-speed train that runs between Paris and Lyon in France, gets its power.

MP3393

The First Voyage of Sinbad
(An Arabic Tale)

Long ago in the city of Baghdad there lived a young man named Sinbad. Although Sinbad loved his city, he wished to travel to new places and make a fortune. So he sold his house and everything he owned. He took the money and bought bundles of goods for trading. He set sail for the East Indies with a group of other merchants.

They sailed for many days when suddenly the wind died. The ship was becalmed, and they had to wait for a fresh wind. The captain told the crew to put out the small life boats and row to a nearby island.

Sinbad found it good to stretch his legs on the island. He helped the other sailors start a fire. The minute the fire was lit, the earth began to heave and shake. Sinbad and the others thought it was an earthquake and ran for their boats. Suddenly the island lifted itself out of the water. Sinbad gasped! It was no island! They had landed on a whale! With one swish of its tail, the whale destroyed Sinbad's little boat and dumped him into the sea. Sinbad grasped a piece of floating timber and hung onto it until morning.

At dawn, Sinbad, now all alone in the sea, saw a real island. He managed to swim to it and drag himself on shore. Some men found him and took him to their king. The king was kind to Sinbad. He gave him food, clothes, and jewels and told Sinbad about life on the island. In return, Sinbad told him many stories about Baghdad.

One day a ship landed on the island. It was the very one on which Sinbad had left Baghdad. The captain, who thought Sinbad had drowned, was very glad to see the young man again. He helped Sinbad find his bundles of goods, which were still packed on the ship. Sinbad gave many fine gifts to the king. He then traded the rest of the goods and made a nice profit. Sinbad thanked the king for his kindness, collected his new wealth, and boarded the merchant ship once again. When the wind came up, Sinbad — richer and wiser — sailed for home.

Main Idea
1. This story is mainly about
   a. a huge whale.
   b. an adventure.
   c. a generous king.

Significant Details
2. Sinbad's home was
   a. on a deserted island.
   b. in the king's palace.
   c. in the city of Baghdad.
3. The earthquake was really
   a. a tidal wave.
   b. the whale moving.
   c. a hurricane.

Context Clues
4. Sinbad made a nice *profit*.
   a. gained more than he spent
   b. large fire on the island
   c. bundle of goods

Drawing Conclusions
5. Which of these statements about the story is surprising?
   a. The wind died down, so the ship stopped.
   b. Sinbad's bundles were still on the ship.
   c. Sinbad was glad to be returning home.

Following Through
6. Was Sinbad brave, lucky, or smart? _____ Explain your answer.
_____
_____
_____
_____
_____
_____

Colin Powell

In 1937, Colin Luther Powell was born in Harlem, New York. His parents, immigrants from Jamaica, looked at their son and knew he would be special. They just didn't know how special.

Colin had an ordinary childhood, growing up in a crowded New York neighborhood. He was not a top-ranking student in school, but he was well-liked. Everyone admired Colin's easy-going ways and ability to get things done. His classmates elected him class president in high school. It wasn't until college, however, that Colin discovered his true interest—the army. Colin noticed an ROTC class (Reserve Officers Training Corps) at City College in New York. The class was practicing precise military drills. Immediately, Colin knew this was for him. Colin joined the ROTC program and worked hard. When he graduated, Colin was at the top of his class and carried the rank of second lieutenant in the army. Colin's brilliant military career as a soldier had begun.

Colin served at many army bases throughout the United States, Europe, Korea, and Vietnam. Everywhere he went, Colin Powell earned the reputation of being dependable, responsible, and loyal. He taught other soldiers to set goals and work hard.

While serving at an army base in Massachusetts, Colin met and married Alma Johnson. But the army soon separated them. Powell was sent to Vietnam where he earned medals for bravery and loyalty. His first son was born while he was in Vietnam.

Back home in the states with his family again, Colin wanted to continue his education. He wanted to earn a master's degree, but was told his grades weren't high enough for graduate school. Determined to get his degree, Colin enrolled in the Army Command and General Staff College in Kansas. Again, he worked extremely hard and graduated second in his class of over 1000 students.

The United States government was beginning to notice this determined officer with a distinguished record of service. By this time, Colin had received the special Soldier's Medal for rescuing his crew members from a fiery helicopter after a crash. He had also earned his master's degree in business administration from George Washington University. The government selected Powell to be a special White House assistant. Only a few military people were chosen for this position, and it was Colin's job to gather information for the president. This job allowed Colin to spend more time with his family, which was growing almost as fast as his military rank was rising. Colin and Alma had three children by then, and Colin had been promoted to major general in the army.

President Ronald Regan personally called Powell and asked him to serve as the National Security Advisor. In this position, Powell had to warn the President about any harm that might come from foreign countries and had to keep the U.S. army ready and alert for defense. This was a tremendous job with great responsibility, but even greater challenges lay ahead.

continued . . .

MP3393

In 1989, Colin Powell became a four-star general, a rank few soldiers ever achieve. That same year, the new president, George Bush, asked General Powell to be the Chairman of the Joint Chiefs of Staff. The Joint Chiefs of Staff is an agency that advises the President on military matters. As Chairman of this committee, Colin Powell became the leader of all of the U.S. armed forces.

His biggest challenge as a military leader came when the country of Iraq invaded the U.S.'s ally, Kuwait. Iraq was ordered to leave Kuwait, but refused. General Powell sent the United States army to Iraq, and the Persian Gulf War, also known as Operation Desert Storm, began. Finally, Iraq surrendered, and the success of the war was attributed to the calm, careful planning of General Powell.

Not long after the war, General Powell retired from military life, but he is still interested in the military and the United States government. He gives lectures and speeches around the country. There is one question his audiences always ask: "How did you become so successful?" And there is one answer that Colin Powell always gives: "Hard work!"

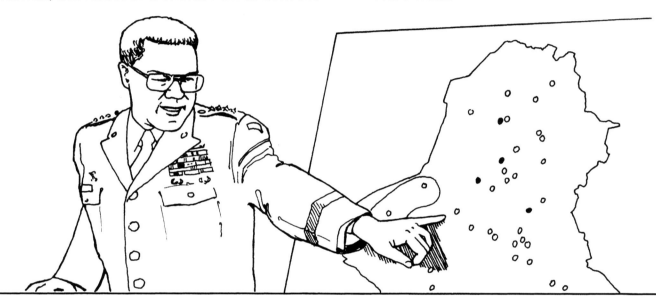

Main Idea

1. Colin Powell is best known as a
   a. student.
   b. president.
   c. soldier.

Significant Details

2. Colin's parents were from
   a. Jamaica.
   b. Massachusetts.
   c. New York.

3. The ROTC program trains people for
   a. government duties.
   b. graduate degrees.
   c. military life.

Context Clues

4. Kuwait is an *ally* of the United States.
   a. enemy
   b. spy
   c. friend

Drawing Conclusions

5. Colin's parents worked hard while Colin was growing up. Give two examples of how Colin applied what he learned from his parents.

_____
_____
_____
_____
_____
_____
_____
_____
_____
_____
_____

Follow Through

6. Read the newspapers and news magazines to find out what Colin Powell is doing now. Make a prediction about his future life.

Fame and Its Price

Have you ever dreamed of seeing your name in lights on Broadway? Do you think your musical ability would make you a good rock star? Are you artistically talented enough to have your work displayed in an art museum?

True, you need talent to accomplish these dreams, but talent isn't all that's needed. Hard work and proper training are necessary to reach any goal. Your local high school may be able to help you get that training.

Many school districts across the country, from Cincinnati to Houston to Los Angeles, have a Visual and Performing Arts Center as part of their program. New York High School of Performing Arts became well known when it was featured in the movie *Fame.* The St. Louis Visual and Performing Arts Center even accepts talented elementary students.

While students at these centers study reading, math, science, and social studies, their main focus is on their chosen art. The centers offer classes in voice training, instrumental music, ballet, tap, jazz, and modern dance, pottery, photography, sculpture, painting and drawing, theater arts, drama techniques, playwriting, and journalism. Sometimes professionals come to the schools to speak to the students, to teach a short course, or to look for new talent.

Because so much time is spent on music, dance, or art, students must be willing to study hard. A dance or theater company will not hire people unless they are skilled in many areas. If you are willing to work for fame and pay its price, a Visual and Performing Arts Center might be an exciting possibility for you.

Significant Details

1. What are three arts you could study at a Visual and Performing Arts Center?
   _____
   _____
   _____

2. Why is the New York High School of Performing Arts well-known?
   _____
   _____

3. If you attend a Visual and Performing Arts Center, what must you be willing to do? _____
   _____
   _____

4. In which city could you attend a Visual and Performing Arts Center in the third grade? _____

Context Clues

5. You must be willing to work for *fame.*
   a. skill
   b. knowledge
   c. to be well known

6. You might choose to study a *visual* art, such as sculpture or painting.
   a. something you can see
   b. something you can practice
   c. something you can write

MP3393

Snowboard Queen

Julie Zell is an extremist. She loves sports that are challenging. Anything fast with a bit of risk-taking and a lot of thrills might appeal to Julie. Her latest and most extreme sport is back-country snowboarding. And, like all her other sports, Julie takes this one to the "extreme."

Snowboarding is an exciting sport. Most snowboarders strap the boards to their boots and perform a series of daring tricks and stunts on a man-made course. But Julie takes this sport a bit farther. Julie is a back-country snowboarder. There are no well-marked courses for her. A helicopter flies Julie and her snowboard high into the mountain tops and drops her in uncharted land. There are no paths, trails, or markers, just boulders, cliffs, steep slopes, and thrills.

Most people would never attempt such a feat, but Julie has done it many times. In fact, she earned the title, "Queen of the Hill" three years in a row.

Perhaps the hardest and most challenging snowboarding competition is in Valdez, Alaska.

The competition is known as "The World Extreme King of the Hill." When snowboarding competitions first began, only men participated. It was thought that young women wouldn't enjoy such a rugged and demanding sport. But Julie had been participating in extreme sports for quite a while. She was born in New York and spent a great deal of time on the ski slopes as a competitive skier. Having mastered the mountains, she next tried the waves. Julie moved to Maui, where the waves are biggest, and learned to surf. She loved the sport and became quite good at it. But again, she was ready for a new challenge. Snowboarding seemed the perfect combination of skiing and surfing. All of her skills came together in this sport, and she became known as the female pioneer of snowboarding. She called attention to the fact that women not only enjoyed, but also excelled at the demanding competition. Julie plans to continue meeting challenges and pushing herself to do her extreme best.

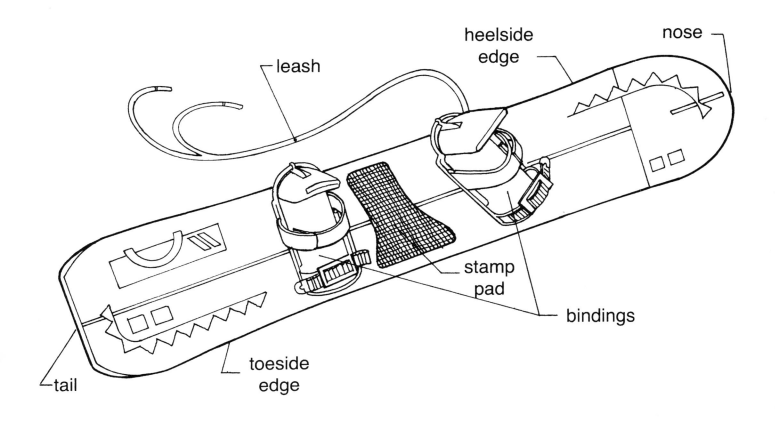

leash

heelside edge

nose

stamp pad

bindings

tail

toeside edge

Main Idea

1. This story is mainly about a woman who
   a. skis.
   b. flies helicopters.
   c. tries challenging sports.

Significant Details

2. Snowboarding is a combination of skiing and
   a. jumping.
   b. surfing.
   c. running.

3. Julie won the title "Queen of the Hill"
   a. her first time in competition.
   b. three times.
   c. at a race in Maui.

Context Clues

4. Julie likes *extreme* sports.
   a. sports in the air
   b. sports with risk and danger
   c. snowsports

Inference

5. If Julie was afraid to try a new sport, she would probably

   a. overcome her fears and try it.
   b. give up.
   c. change the sport so it would be easier for her.

Drawing Conclusions

6. Julie is called a pioneer of snowboarders because
   a. she was the first one to ever try the sport.
   b. she lived in the woods and mountains like pioneers.
   c. she was one of the first females to bring attention to the sport.

Follow Through

7. Think of a time when you challenged yourself to go to the extreme. Tell about it. If you have not had such an experience, tell about something you would like to try or master. Explain what you would have to do to be your best.

_____

_____

_____

_____

43

MP3393

Jackie Joyner-Kersee

It is hard to imagine someone jumping a distance of 24 feet. That's farther than the length of an average van. Yet Jackie Joyner-Kersee did it with a smile. Jackie, one of four children, grew up in East St. Louis, Illinois. As a young girl, she focused on school and sports.

Jackie is a strong person, physically and mentally. She has also been fortunate enough to be given good advice throughout her life. Her mother, Mary, insisted on good school work. Her brother, Al, matched Jackie's love of sports. He gave her constant encouragement as well as competition. Later, her husband and coach, Bob Kersee, turned her toward world championships.

Jackie attended college at UCLA, where she met Coach Kersee. He saw that Jackie had great skill and talent.

With his encouragement and guidance, Jackie began competing in the World Heptathlon events. These are a combination of seven running, jumping, and throwing sports events.

Her mental attitude toward sports and her physical power have resulted in wonderful performances. In 1987, Jackie won both the heptathlon and long jump at the World Track and Field Championships. This ranked her as the best all-around woman athlete in the world. Jackie went on to win an Olympic Gold Medal for the long jump in 1988 and a Bronze Medal in 1992.

Jackie gives much of her time and attention to disadvantaged children, as well as to senior citizens. She encourages them to try anything, just as her family encouraged her. Jackie has gone far beyond what her family hoped for her, and much of her success is based on what they taught her.

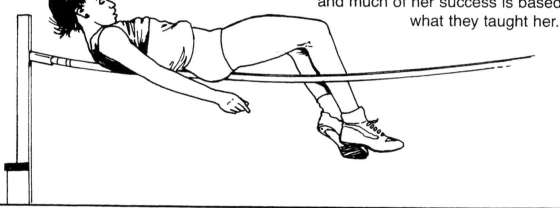

Main Idea

1. This story is mainly about a(n)
   a. coach.
   b. sporting event.
   c. athlete.

Significant Details

2. Jackie grew up in
   a. St. Louis.
   b. Illinois.
   c. California.

3. How many events are featured in a heptathlon?
   a. one hundred
   b. twenty-four
   c. seven

4. Jackie's coach is also her
   a. brother.
   b. husband.
   c. college teammate.

Context Clues

5. Jackie's mother *insisted* on good school performance.
   a. demanded
   b. let her relax
   c. was proud of

Drawing Conclusions

6. From the story you can tell that Jackie enters sports events because
   a. her husband wants her to win.
   b. she likes to compete.
   c. she likes to travel.